Skin & Nails
Care Tips for Girls

By Julie Williams

Illustrated by Shawn Banner

American★Girl®

Published by Pleasant Company Publications

Questions or comments?
Call 1-800-845-0005, or write
American Girl, P.O. Box 620497, Middleton, WI 53562-0497.

Visit our Web site at **americangirl.com**.

Printed in China.
04 05 06 07 08 09 LEO 10 9 8 7 6 5 4

American Girl® and American Girl Library® are registered trademarks
of American Girl, LLC.

Editorial Development: Elizabeth Chobanian, Michelle Watkins

Art Direction & Design: Chris Lorette David

Production: Kendra Pulvermacher, Mindy Rappe, Jeannette Bailey

Illustrations: Shawn Banner

Model Photography: Sandy May

Nail Photography: Jamie Young

Nail Styling: Theresa Lawrence

This book is not intended to replace the advice of or treatment by physicians.
Questions or concerns about physical health should always be discussed
with a doctor. All the instructions in this book have been tested. Results from
testing were incorporated into this book. Nonetheless, all recommendations
and suggestions are made without any guarantees on the part of Pleasant
Company Publications. Because of differing tools, ingredients, conditions,
and individual skills, the publisher disclaims liability for any injuries, losses,
or other damages that may result from using the information in this book.

Library of Congress Cataloging-in Publication Data

Williams, Julie.
Skin and nails : care tips for girls / by Julie Williams ;
illustrated by Shawn Banner.
p. cm.
Summary: A basic guide to skin and nail care, including healthy habits,
sun protection, and personal hygiene, as well as products to buy or make,
manicures for every mood, and ideas for a spa party to pamper oneself and
one's friends.
ISBN 1-58485-793-5
[1. Skin—Care and anatomy. 2. Nails (anatomy)—Care and hygiene.
3. Girls—Health and hygiene.] I. Banner, Shawn, ill. II. Title.

RL87 . W715 2003
646.7/26/08342—dc 21   2003043312

Want to have a **healthy, natural glow? Clean, clear skin? Strong, smooth nails?** Here's how to care for your skin from head to toe. Learn how to . . .

- put your best face forward with a **facial,**
- make your own **beauty potions,**
- have **fun in the sun**—without the burn,
- keep your **nails nice and neat,** and
- give your **feet** a treat.

You'll also find fun ideas for **painting your nails to match your mood** and throwing a **spa party** to pamper yourself and your friends.

Your friends at American Girl

Contents

Skin Smarts

Hands & Feet

Ooh-La-La Spa Party

Skin Smarts

Get to know the skin you're in, and give it the care it needs to stay clean and clear.

7 Secrets to Beautiful

Make habits of these simple body-care basics.

1 Clean It

Your skin secretes oil and sheds dead cells. Prevent this soil and oil from building up by getting into a **daily cleansing routine.**

2 Feed It

Eat lots of fruits, veggies, and whole-grain foods to give your body the vitamins and nutrients it needs to make healthy skin.

3 Work It

Run, jump, walk, ride. No matter which activity you choose, regular exercise gets your blood pumping so that it can deliver oxygen and nutrients to your skin. Exercise also helps you get rid of stress, which can cause your skin to break out or become irritated.

Skin

4 Water It

Drink up! Have at least *eight glasses of water daily* to keep your skin hydrated and moist. (Sorry. Soda doesn't count.)

5 Protect It

Sun damage is your skin's invisible enemy. Squirt on *sunscreen*, hide your head under a *hat*, and protect your lips with a *high-SPF lip balm* before enjoying any rays.

6 Rest It

Get your beauty rest. Tuck in for *at least eight hours of sleep* a night to give your body and skin a chance to rejuvenate and repair themselves.

7 Pamper It

Make time for freshening facials and soothing soaks in the tub. *Special treatments* will relax and refresh and will give you a healthy glow.

What's Your Skin Type?

Skin comes in four basic types: oily, dry, normal, and combination. Find out which kind you have and how to care for it.

1. You get pimples . . .

   a. all the time.

   b. often on oilier places on your face but hardly ever elsewhere.

   c. every now and then.

   d. never.

2. When you wake up in the morning, your face feels . . .

   a. greasy.

   b. oily in some places, dry or normal in others.

   c. smooth and soft.

   d. itchy and tight.

3. An hour or two after washing your face, your skin looks . . .

   a. shiny all over.

   b. shiny in some places and flaky in others.

   c. fresh and clean.

   d. flaky, red, or ashy.

If you answered . . .

Mostly a's

You have oily skin. Why the extra shine? The glands under your skin produce more oil than your face needs to stay moist.

Clean Routine: Wash your face with a mild soap or cleanser and warm water to break down the oil on your face. Apply a toner or astringent after washing to help zap the grease and tighten pores. Look for products that are oil-free. During the day, try blotting your face with disposable tissues made especially to soak up oil.

Mostly b's

You have combination skin. It's oily in the T-zone (the forehead, nose, and chin) and dry or normal on the cheeks and other areas.

Clean Routine: Wash your face with a mild soap or cleanser. After washing, treat each area differently: use a light moisturizer on dry areas and apply a toner to the oily areas.

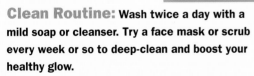

Mostly c's

You have normal skin. Lucky you! But even a smooth, clear complexion needs good care.

Clean Routine: Wash twice a day with a mild soap or cleanser. Try a face mask or scrub every week or so to deep-clean and boost your healthy glow.

Mostly d's

You have dry skin. Your skin needs more moisture to keep it from being flaky, red, or ashy.

Clean Routine: Wash your face with gentle, soap-free cleanser that doesn't dry your face out any further. You may want to try a light moisturizer after cleansing. Stay away from toner, but use a moisturizing facial mask once a week to remove the dull, dry cells on the surface of your skin.

Beauty Shop

Masks are thick mixtures that you leave on the face for a period of time. When removed, they lift dead cells from your skin.

An **exfoliant** is a product that removes dead skin cells. Scrubs and masks are examples of exfoliants.

Toners remove oil from the surface of your skin and tighten pores. They are also called astringents, clarifying lotions, or skin purifiers.

The sandy or rough texture of a **scrub** helps loosen dead cells and smooth the skin's surface.

Moisturizers help keep moisture in your skin. They range from light lotions to thick creams.

Wondering what all the different products do? Here's a quick guide to some of the skin-care choices you'll find on store shelves.

Oil-free products don't contain any oil that can lead to blocked pores and blemishes.

Since soap can irritate sensitive skin, **soap-free** cleansers use other ingredients to clean skin gently.

Noncomedogenic products won't clog pores.

13

Suds Up!

Know which cleanser is right for your face.

The Scoop on Soap

It's best to wash your face with a mild soap or cleanser that doesn't contain any special deodorants, moisturizers, or other ingredients that may irritate your skin. You may also want to keep your own bar of face soap tucked away for your use only. Sharing soap with the whole family will spread unwanted germs to your face. Same goes for your towel. Make sure it's clean and dry—and yours alone.

Super Sensitive?

If your face tends to break out often, gets extra dry, or burns and gets irritated after you put anything on it, you may have sensitive skin. Look for a cleanser or soap that is *hypoallergenic*—meaning that it has been tested and found to be free of any ingredients that may cause allergies. Products that are noncomedogenic won't clog pores. If your skin feels really tight and dry after washing, you may also be sensitive to soap itself. Try using a soap-free cleanser.

Caution!

Always test products, whether from a store or made at home, on a small area on the inside of your wrist before using them on your face. That way, if your skin reacts, you'll know the product isn't right for you.

Face Care

The skin on your face is softer, smoother, and more sensitive than the skin on any other part of your body, and it needs special care.

Clean Routine

Wash your face twice a day— once in the morning and once at night. You should never go to bed without washing away the day's dirt, no matter how tired you are.

Five Steps to a Fresh Face

1 Get Set. Sweep your hair off your face with a headband or barrette.

2 Get Wet. Splash your face with warm water. (Test the water with your finger before splashing it onto your face. If the water stings your finger, it's too hot.)

3 Suds Up. Rub a mild cleanser in the palms of your hands. You may be tempted to use a washcloth, but the safest and softest tools are your hands. Use your fingertips to work the cleanser onto your face in a circular motion. Don't forget to wash under your chin and around your hairline.

4 Rinse Off. Splash warm water over your face to rinse the suds away. Keep splashing until all the cleanser is rinsed off.

5 **Dab Dry.** Gently pat your face dry (never rub!) with a clean towel.

Bathing Beauty

Soak up good vibes and soothing scents in the tub.

The Ultimate Soak

1   **Run water** into tub. Test the water temperature with your fingers to make sure it's not too hot.

2   Close the drain and **add a magical mixer** of your choice to the water. Soap in your bath may lead to urinary tract infections or irritations, so stay away from cleansers and bubble baths when taking a soak.

3   When the tub is half full, turn off the water and **slide in slowly.** If the water feels too hot at first, cool it by running a little cold water into the tub.

4   Lie back, **relax,** take a deep breath . . . ahh!

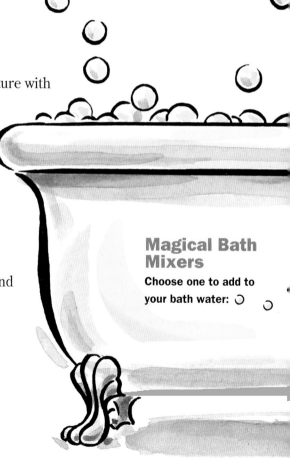

Magical Bath Mixers

Choose one to add to your bath water:

5 When you're ready to get out, open the drain and let the water run out. As the tub empties, stand up and **shower** to rinse any remaining suds or salts off your skin.

6 **Pat dry** with a fresh, clean towel.

- 2 cups powdered milk
- 2 tablespoons rose water plus fresh rose petals
- A few moisturizing bath oil beads
- A handful of bath crystals or salts
- A fizzy bath bomb

Beauty Potions

Whip up a do-it-yourself skin-care concoction to deep-clean your face and body. (Always remember to wash your skin before using a potion.)

Oatmeal Smoothie
(for your face*)

Ooh! Your skin will feel so soft after using this scrub.
*normal/combination/oily skin

3 tablespoons old-fashioned (not instant) oatmeal, uncooked

2 tablespoons plain yogurt

Mix oatmeal and yogurt into a paste and pat onto your face. Hang out for 15 minutes. Rinse off with warm water.

★ Always keep masks and scrubs away from the area around your eyes!

Important!
Chunks of oatmeal or banana can clog plumbing. Remember to clean the sink and drain when you're done!

Papaya Mask
(for your face*)

The natural juices in papaya clean and moisturize.

*normal/dry skin

1/2 papaya

Lightly mash half a papaya in a bowl with a fork or your fingers. Rub the papaya over your face. Let the fruit dry, about 10 minutes. Rinse off with warm water.

Banana Mash Mask
(for your face*)

Bananas give your face a special treat.

*all skin types

1 ripe banana

1 teaspoon honey

Mash the banana in a bowl with a fork. (Don't overmash or it will become too runny.) Mix in the honey. Spread the mask onto your face and let it sit for 10 minutes. Rinse clean with lukewarm water.

Sugar Scrub
(for your body)

Give your skin a sweet treat to polish away dead skin cells.

3 tablespoons sugar   **2 tablespoons baby oil**

Mix sugar and oil to make a paste. Moisten your skin in the shower. Then, standing clear of the water, rub the scrub in a circular motion all over your body. (Do *not* use scrub on your face.) Rinse with warm water.

Pamper Your Face

Treat yourself to a salon-style facial.

1 Get Set

Turn on some soothing music to get relaxed. Wrap yourself in a robe. Pull your hair away from your face and secure with a hairband or scrunchie. Place a towel around your neck.

2 Warm Up

Soak a washcloth in very warm water and hold it against your face. This will warm and moisten your skin.

3 Cleanse

Wash your face with cleanser or soap to remove any dirt. Pat face dry with a towel.

4 Deep-Clean

Next, apply a mask or use a scrub appropriate for your skin type to help remove any stubborn dead skin cells or other impurities from your face.

5 Relax

While you're waiting for the mask to dry, find a comfy place to sit or lie back. Close your eyes and place cucumber or potato slices on your lids to soothe them. When the mask is dry, rinse it off your face.

6 Tingle

Next, put a bit of toner on a cotton ball and apply it to your face in a circular motion. You should get a cool, refreshing sensation as the toner clears your skin of dead cells, oils, and any leftover soap.

7 Soften

Pour a small amount of moisturizing lotion in the palm of your hand. Apply to your face and let the moisturizer sink in.

8 Massage

Move your fingers over your skin in a light, circular motion. This will help relax the muscles in your face. Finish by tapping your fingertips lightly and quickly all over your face to awaken the nerves in your skin.

Now you're ready to put your best face forward.

Hello, Sunshine!

Soaking up the sun may feel good and brighten your spirits, but those rays will also damage your skin over time. Here's how to play it smart.

Nice Tan?

Don't be so sure. The sun showers your body with invisible, harmful ultraviolet (UV) rays. When these rays penetrate your skin, they cause it to change color, giving you a tan or, in some cases, a sunburn. Over time, exposure to UV rays can lead to freckles, brown spots, wrinkles, and even skin cancer—not to mention early aging of the skin. Not so nice, huh?

Screen It Out

How can you have fun in the sun without damaging your skin? Apply sunscreen lotion with a sun protection factor (SPF) of at least 30 about 20 minutes *before* going outside. Sunscreen will help reflect some of the harmful rays and prevent burning. If you have skin that breaks out often, use an oil-free, hypoallergenic sunscreen on your face to avoid irritation. Reapply sunscreen generously as often as once an hour or after swimming or exercise—even if the lotion is waterproof.

Anytime, Anywhere

Don't underestimate the power of the sun. You can get just as much sun exposure on a cloudy day as you can on a clear day—and in winter as well as summer. So whether you're building a snow fort or a sand castle, get into the habit of using sunscreen whenever you're outside. And take extra care in covering up between 10 A.M. and 3 P.M., when the sun is strongest.

Never Too Young

Did you know that before you turn 18, you'll soak up about two-thirds of the total amount of UV rays you'll get in your whole lifetime? Be sun smart now, when it matters most.

Sun Survival Guide

How to protect yourself at the beach, and what to do if you still go home with a burn

Voted Most Likely to Burn

Pay special attention to these most often forgotten spots when applying sunscreen.

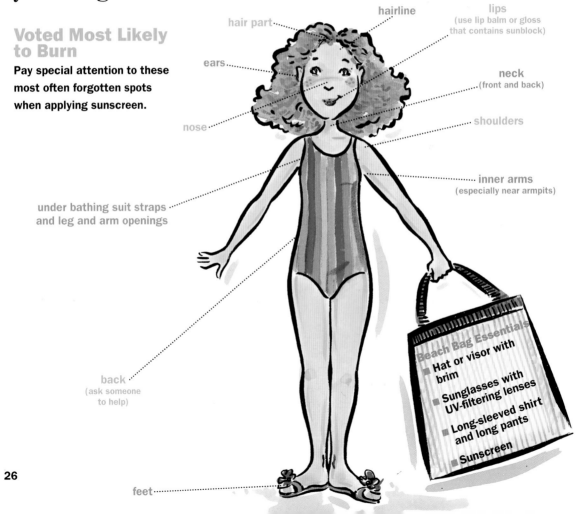

hair part

hairline

lips
(use lip balm or gloss that contains sunblock)

ears

nose

neck
(front and back)

shoulders

inner arms
(especially near armpits)

under bathing suit straps and leg and arm openings

back
(ask someone to help)

feet

Beach Bag Essentials

■ Hat or visor with brim

■ Sunglasses with UV-filtering lenses

■ Long-sleeved shirt and long pants

■ Sunscreen

Got Freckles?

Exposure to the sun can make freckles multiply and darken. Cover your freckled areas with a hat or clothing, and always use sunscreen.

Baked?

Quench your sunburned skin with a cold compress or a cool shower or bath. Then apply lotion to soothe and protect. Use your regular lotion or try an aloe vera gel, which will help your skin naturally heal. (Keep a bottle in the fridge for a cool sensation when you put it on.) Have an adult give you ibuprofen to ease the pain. Wear loose clothing that doesn't rub against your skin and irritate the burn. And if your skin starts to peel, don't help the process along with your fingers—let the skin come off by itself when you shower or bathe. If large areas are blistered and peeling, call your doctor.

Don't Sweat It

Perspiration is good for your skin.

Keepin' Cool

Everyone sweats. Sweating is your body's natural way of keeping cool. When your body heats up during exercise or hot weather, your skin releases sweat from its pores. So when the next breeze comes by, evaporation is bound to cool you. Dirt, toxins, and pollutants that are resting in the pores also get flushed out when you sweat, making for cleaner skin.

P.U.! B.O.

You can prevent body odor by bathing regularly and by wearing deodorant. Apply it to your armpits every morning to keep smelling fresh all day. To prevent wet circles under your arms, look for a deodorant that also contains *antiperspirant,* which will help cut down on the amount of sweat.

Shower Time

Depending on how dirty or sweaty you get, you'll want to wash the skin on your body once a day or every other day. Use warm water (never hot because it could dry out your skin) and soap or liquid body wash to cleanse away the oils, sweat, and dirt on your skin. Pay special attention to areas of your body where you perspire most, like your armpits, forehead, and feet.

Play It Fresh

If you're a sporty girl, protect your skin with a sweatproof sunscreen. It's specially made to keep your hands from feeling slippery, and it won't drip off with your sweat. Wear a headband to keep sweat beads from stinging your eyes or a wristband to wipe your brow. You'll want to shower or bathe after sports or exercise in order to clean any dried sweat from your skin. And be sure to wash sweaty clothing before wearing it again.

Ugh! Pimples!

As you get older, your body produces more oil, which combines with bacteria and dead skin cells to clog your pores—and that causes pimples. Here are some tips on dealing with zits.

Hands Off!

The best thing to do with a pimple is to leave it alone.
Don't touch it. **Don't** squeeze it. **Don't** pick it. **Don't** pop it.

Be Patient

Wash your face as you normally do and give the pimple time to run its course. To speed up the drying process, however, you may try dabbing on an acne cream that contains benzoyl peroxide. But this cream may cause the skin around the pimple to become dry and itchy, so you'll need to summon all your superpowers to keep from scratching or picking at it.

Touch and Go

Do the areas of skin around your mouth, nose, chin, and cheek break out more than the rest of your face? That's not surprising. You touch those spots the most. Think about when your hands find their way to your face without your knowing it. During a spelling test? While watching TV? During chats on the phone? Try to break the habit by keeping your fingers otherwise occupied. Keep a small toy in your pocket to fiddle with, or sit on your hands.

Bang Breakouts

Do you break out where your bangs touch your face? Oil from your hair is the likely cause. Use a headband or barrettes to pull your hair away from your face. And wash your hair often enough to control oiliness.

Too Embarrassed to Be Seen?

There's no reason to be ashamed of a pimple on your face. Everyone gets one from time to time. But if you really must save face, cover the spot with a medicated concealer. Look for one that is **noncomedogenic** so it won't clog your pores as it conceals.

Be sure to wash the concealer off your face before going to bed. If over-the-counter products don't help, see your doctor for more advice. There are many acne medications that might help.

Face the Facts

Answer the questions below to find out if you're the victim of a zit myth.

1. Eating chocolate causes breakouts.
Yeah!   **Not!**

2. Tanning helps clear up pimples.
True   **False**

3. Squeezing a pimple will make it go away.
Yep   **No way!**

4. You should wash and scrub your face frequently to prevent pimples.
Of course   **Nope**

5. For a quick pimple fix, put a dab of toothpaste on your zit.
Why not?   **Forget it!**

6. The best way to get rid of a zit is to leave it untreated.
Yes   **No**

Answers

1. **Not!** No food has been found to directly cause break-outs. But a nutritious diet is important for good health—and that makes for great skin.

2. **False.** Sorry. It's simply not true that the sun will help heal your zits. In fact, the sun may make your face oilier, and some acne medications may make your face more susceptible to sun damage.

3. **No way!** In fact, squeezing a pimple will only make it more inflamed and may lead to infection. Your fingers may also help spread germs to areas nearby.

4. **Nope.** When you wash your face, you remove some of the oils that help keep your face soft and moist. If you wash too often, your face will have no oils and become dry. This, in turn, will convince those glands to get to work and make more oil. And scrubbing will only irritate your poor skin even more.

5. **Forget it!** It's true that a dab of toothpaste will dry up a pimple, but it will also make the skin dry and flaky and call for more TLC.

6. **Yes and no.** In most cases, letting a pimple run its normal course is the best way to go. But if you have a lot of inflamed, swollen areas with a number of zits on your face, you may need to see a *dermatologist,* a doctor who can help treat skin problems.

33

Hands & Feet

Make your hands and feet look and feel great with just the right care.

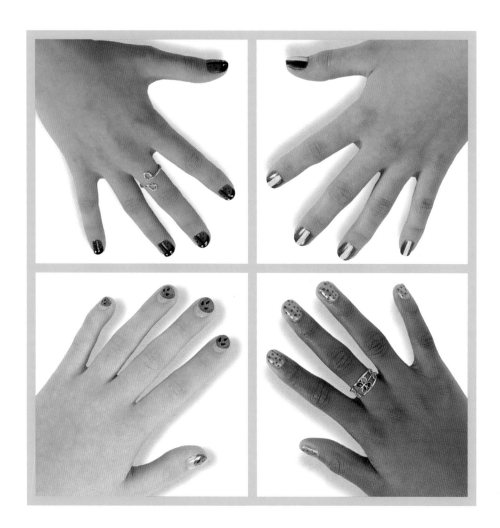

What Do Your Nails Say about You?

Pick the answer that fits you best.

1. Darn! You broke a nail. That's the second time . . .

   a. in four months.

   b. in the past month.

   c. this week.

2. The last time you rubbed lotion onto your hands was . . .

   a. this morning.

   b. about a week or two ago.

   c. too long ago to remember.

3. When a friend grabs your hand during gym class, she says . . .

   a. "Ooh, I love your nails!"

   b. "Hold on tight!"

   c. "Are you still biting your nails?"

4. When you pay for your new shirt at Unlimited Three, the salesperson presents you with a scratch-off sweepstakes card. You . . .

   a. find a penny to scratch off the coating.

   b. scratch off the coating with a fingernail.

   c. try to scratch off the coating with a fingernail . . . but can't because your nails are too short.

5. Painting your nails makes you feel . . .

    a. polished, pretty, and pampered.

    b. nervous. You don't have much practice at it, and you always make a mess.

    c. silly. What's the point? You'll peel off the polish as soon as it dries.

6. Summer's here and it's time to break out the sandals. You . . .

    a. paint your toenails so your feet will look great.

    b. slip on your flip-flops and dash outside without giving a thought to what your toes look like.

    c. wear tennis shoes instead 'cause your feet are a terrible sight.

Answers
If you answered . . .

Mostly a's
Nice 'n' Neat

You pamper your hands and nails. You're careful about how you use them and you keep them looking and feeling great. Painting your nails is a frequent treat. Keep up the good grooming and reward yourself with a new polish style from these pages or a soothing foot cream.

Mostly b's
Plain 'n' Practical

You're a practical girl who doesn't go out of her way to pamper her hands. You keep your nails short and unpolished because it's just easier that way. Sure, you'll moisturize and trim, but only when chips, tears, and dryness make it necessary. Instead of waiting for something bad to happen, try a manicure every few weeks to prevent hand and nail emergencies.

Mostly c's
Used 'n' Abused

Hand lotion is a rare treat, and a polish or trim doesn't even register on your radar screen. Your hands are invisible to you— that is, until you have to show them to others. Then you probably secretly wish you had neat hands and nails. Start with a basic trim and moisturize from time to time. Then you'll see that even just a little TLC leads to smoother, softer hands.

5 Keys to Healthy Hands

Unlock the secrets to keeping your hardworking hands happy.

1 Lather Up

Because your hands go everywhere and touch so much, they pick up lots of bacteria and dirt. Keep hands squeaky clean and germfree by washing with soap and warm water often—after using the bathroom, before and after handling food, after playing with your pet, after tossing a ball in the backyard, and especially after catching a sneeze or blowing your nose. And really wash them; don't just hold them under running water for a second. Work up a lather. Wash the backs of your hands, between your fingers, and even your wrists. If you're on the go, take along a bottle of antibacterial hand gel to tide you over until you can get to a sink.

2 Soften Up

When you wash your hands, the soap removes not only the dirt and germs but also the oils from your skin. No oil means dry skin. Add the moisture back in by rubbing on hand lotion at least once a day.

3 Trim Up

Keep an eye on your nails. Trim or file them if they get too long. Use a nailbrush to gently scrub dirt out from under them. And take care of any chips, tears, or rough edges on nails as soon as they happen.

4 Cover Up

Cleaning products, harsh weather, extreme temperatures, and even some sports wreak havoc on hands. Consider wearing work gloves when doing heavy-duty work—such as washing the car, gardening, and raking leaves. Wear rubber gloves during long stints at the kitchen sink washing pots and pans. Cuddle your hands in a pair of gloves or mittens before going outside in the wintertime, and cushion hands with sport gloves before a long bike ride.

5 Screen Out

Yep, the sun hits those hands, too. When you slather sunscreen on your face and body, don't forget to add some to the backs of your hands.

Help for Nails

Do your nails break, chip, or tear? Here's what to do when nail care gets tricky.

Hangnails

You have a little piece of skin hanging near your nail. It hurts like crazy every time you touch it, bump it, or even look at it!

Ouch! You have a *hangnail,* a torn piece of skin near the nail caused by dryness. A hangnail can be very painful, especially if you pick or bite at it—so don't! Instead, use nail clippers to cut the hangnail off as close to the skin as possible. Then apply a dab of antibacterial ointment to make sure it doesn't get infected. It's also best to wait a day or two for the damaged area to heal before applying polish. You can try to prevent hangnails by massaging hand lotion into the skin around your nails to prevent the skin from drying out and tearing.

White Spots

Sometimes you get funny little white spots under your fingernails. What's the deal?

Like brittleness, white spots can also be caused by poor nutrition, so make sure you're eating lots of fruits, vegetables, and whole-grain foods. White spots can also be a sign of damage to the nail bed caused while cleaning under your nail. Go easy with the nail brush, and don't use any hard objects or a metal file to clean under your nails. The good news about white spots is that they'll eventually grow out.

Yellow Nails

Whenever you take off your nail polish, your nails underneath are an icky yellow color. Is this normal?

If you polish your nails a lot, yes. Yellowing is caused by harsh dyes in the polish. Give your nails a break and go with a natural look for a while. You can also soak nails in lemon juice for five minutes to whiten them. When you do paint your nails again, apply a base coat of clear polish to protect the nails from the dyes. Better yet, look for polish in a non-yellowing formula.

Critical Cuticles

Your cuticles are so thick and gross you're embarrassed to show your hands. Can you do something about them?

A cuticle acts as a seal between your nail and the rest of the skin on your finger. It prevents dirt and bacteria from getting below the nail. Keep cuticles up to the task with a bit of extra care. First, soften your cuticles by rubbing hand lotion, cuticle cream, or cuticle oil into them. Then, after a bath or shower, use a wet washcloth and *gently* push cuticles back off the nail. Steer clear of orangewood sticks and cuticle tools—they're not as gentle as a washcloth. Whatever you do, don't cut your cuticles. You could damage the seal and risk infection.

Habit Busters

Situation 1

You **bite or pick** at your nails while . . .	What's Up?	Solution
. . . watching TV or a movie. . . . reading something you'd rather not. . . . riding in a car.	You're bored.	Find something else to do with your hands to keep them busy and out of your mouth— bounce a rubber ball, braid your hair, doodle, learn sign language, or even just stick your hands in your pockets.

Situation 2

You **bite or pick** at your nails while . . .	What's Up?	Solution
. . . taking a test. . . . waiting in the doctor's office. . . . watching a really close basketball game.	You're nervous or stressed out.	Take a deep breath, do some simple stretches, or go for a walk to work off that nervous energy in a healthier way.

Bite or pick at your nails? You *can* stop. First, figure out when and why you do it. Find the situation that best describes when you're most likely to be caught red-handed.

Situation 3

You bite or pick at your nails while . . .	What's Up?	Solution
. . . you just broke a nail and are left with a sharp, jagged edge. . . . that darn chip in your nail keeps catching on your new sweater.	You need to trim your nails pronto!—before anyone gets hurt or that new sweater unravels.	There are tools for trimming and shaping your nails, so please don't use your teeth. Keep clippers and an emery board close by so you can reach for them on demand.

Situation 4

You bite or pick at your nails while . . .	What's Up?	Solution
. . . who knows? You don't realize you're doing it until it's too late.	Maybe you just like to have something in your mouth. It makes you feel secure, like a baby with a bottle.	Chew a piece of gum, lick a lollipop, or nibble a piece of licorice.

More Ways to Give Your Nails a Break

- Reward yourself. Put a quarter into a piggy bank every day you don't bite your nails. When you quit for good, you get to crack open the bank.

- Find a partner. Ask a friend with the same problem to quit with you.

- Put on gloves or mittens when you're at home—especially if you bite your nails in your sleep.

- Give yourself a really nice manicure. Having pretty nails could be just the thing to keep you from wanting to bite them.

Nail Shop

Here are the tools for smart hand and foot care.

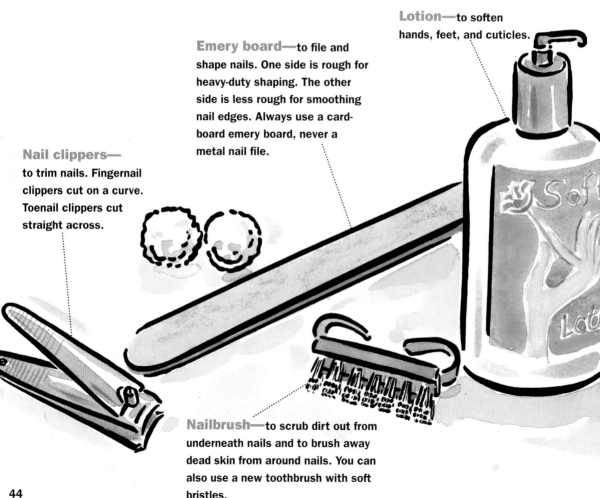

Lotion—to soften hands, feet, and cuticles.

Emery board—to file and shape nails. One side is rough for heavy-duty shaping. The other side is less rough for smoothing nail edges. Always use a cardboard emery board, never a metal nail file.

Nail clippers—to trim nails. Fingernail clippers cut on a curve. Toenail clippers cut straight across.

Nailbrush—to scrub dirt out from underneath nails and to brush away dead skin from around nails. You can also use a new toothbrush with soft bristles.

Polish—to paint your nails. You may want to start with a base coat of clear polish to protect the nail and finish with a clear topcoat to protect the polish.

Nail buffer—to smooth and shine up the surface of the nails. A buffer is shaped like an emery board, but it has three different surfaces to work with. Use only the softest, grit-free side to shine your nails.

Polish remover—to remove polish from nails. Be sure to use an acetone-free formula that won't dry your nails.

Toe separator—keeps toes separated while you polish toenails. You can also use crunched-up tissues or cotton balls between your toes.

Cotton balls or pads—to use with polish remover to wipe polish from nails and clean up mistakes.

In Your Hands

Be nice to your nails! Shape and shine them every few weeks with a basic manicure.

1 Get Set

Pick a place for your manicure that is near a sink. Gather all the equipment listed at left, and place it on a countertop or table-top covered with paper towels. Put the bowl of warm water in the middle of your work area, and lay the hand towel in front.

2 Clean

Remove any old polish from your nails. Moisten a cotton ball with remover and place it on a nail, hold it there for a few seconds, then wipe off the polish. Repeat with other nails. Wash hands and nails with warm water and soap.

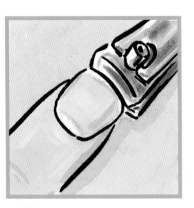

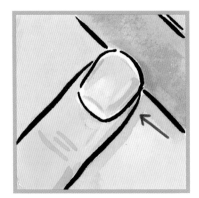

3 Trim

If your nails are too long, use a pair of nail clippers to trim them to the length you want. Be careful not to cut them too short—never below the white part—and ask an adult to help.

4 Shape

Once your nails are the right length, shape them into squared-off ovals by moving the emery board over the edges of your nails in short, quick motions. File in one direction—not back and forth. Always slide the board away from the nail, not toward it. Never use an emery board when nails are wet and more likely to tear or chip.

5 Soak

Place your fingers in a bowl filled with warm, sudsy water and let them soak. This will cleanse and moisten your fingers, nails, and cuticles. When 5 minutes are up, dry your hands with the towel.

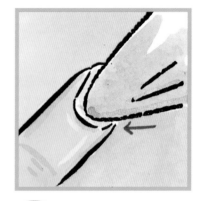

Brush

Rub the nailbrush under the white parts of your nails to remove dirt. Rinse hands.

7 Soften

Wet the washcloths in warm water. Squeeze a dime-sized dollop of hand lotion onto your hands and rub it into your skin and cuticles. Wrap the moist washcloths around your hands and wait for 1 minute while your skin absorbs the lotion and moisture.

8 Cuticle Care

Now that your hands are soft and moist, take care of the skin around your nails—your cuticles. Loosely wrap a finger in a damp washcloth and *gently* push the cuticle back from the nail. Repeat for each finger. (Never cut cuticles—that could lead to infection—and stay away from cuticle sticks.)

Buff

- Rub the softest side of the buffer against the edges of your nails to smooth out any bumps.

- Then rub the buffer across the tops of your nails to give them a light shine. Rinse off any dust that collects along the sides of your nails.

- For extra moisturizing, rub a tiny bit of olive or baby oil onto and around your nails.

9 Shine

Once you've cleaned and shaped your nails and softened your cuticles, you're ready to polish. There are two ways you can give your nails a healthy shine: you can rub them with a nail buffer for a natural look, or you can paint them with nail polish for a colorful finish.

Paint

- Before opening, roll the bottle of polish between your palms to mix it. Remove the brush and dab excess drops of polish on the inside lip of the bottle.

- First, paint a strip of polish onto the middle of your nail. Then paint a strip on each side of the first strip to coat the nail. Repeat on other nails. Let polish dry (this should take about 4 or 5 minutes), then repeat with a second coat.

10 Tips
Painting pointers for smudge-proof nails

Apply polish in
thin coats.

Always apply the first
brushstroke in the
middle of the
nail.

Paint one hand at
a time to cut down on
smudges, and let it dry
before starting the other.

Roll the bottle of
polish between your
palms to mix it well and
avoid air bubbles.

Team up with a friend
or adult to paint each other's
nails. You'll especially appre-
ciate the help when it comes
to painting the nails on the
hand you write with.

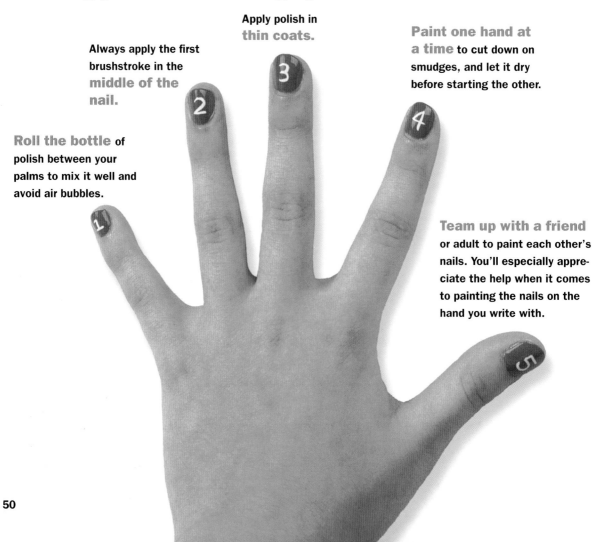

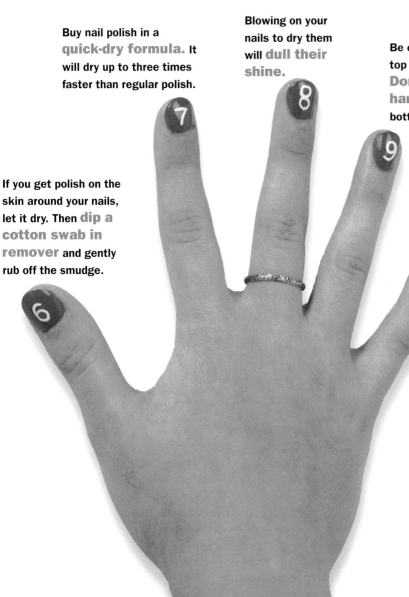

Buy nail polish in a **quick-dry formula.** It will dry up to three times faster than regular polish.

Blowing on your nails to dry them will **dull their shine.**

Be careful when polishing on top of another dry coat. **Don't press down too hard,** or you'll dissolve the bottom layer of polish.

If you get polish on the skin around your nails, let it dry. Then **dip a cotton swab in remover** and gently rub off the smudge.

Prevent goopy polish by storing bottles in the refrigerator.

Safe Painting

Nail polish is strong-smelling stuff. Always paint your nails in a well-aired room, not in an enclosed space. Always work on a protected surface. Keep nail polish and remover away from children ages eight and under. And don't forget to screw the caps back on!

51

Fun Fingernails

Bright and bold, or pretty and pastel? Pick a style that fits your mood and paint away.

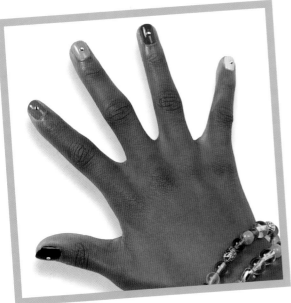

Rainbow Rhinestones

Paint each of your nails a different color. Before the polish dries, place a rhinestone in the middle of each nail. After the first coat dries, finish with a second coat of clear polish.

Sporty Stripes

Paint your nails with a base color. When it dries, paint a stripe of a different color down the middle of each nail.

Polka Dotty

Paint each of your nails with a base color. Let dry completely. Using a different color of polish, add polka dots with a toothpick.

Gel Art

Paint each nail with a dark polish. Wait at least 2 to 3 hours for the polish to dry. Then, draw or write on each nail with a gel pen. Finish with a coat of clear polish.

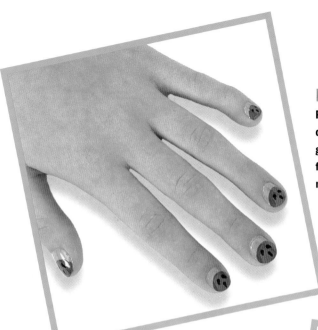

Melon Tips

Paint your nails with watermelon pink polish. Let dry completely. Using a small brush, paint a lime green crescent at the base of each nail. Use a fine-tipped paintbrush dipped in black polish to make seeds.

Sun and Sky

Paint all your nails blue. Let dry. Then, one nail at a time, add a second, thicker coat of blue, but before it dries, dab white polish on the nail and swirl with a toothpick. Paint a yellow sun on your thumbnail.

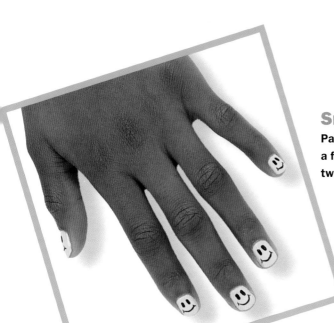

Smiley Faces

Paint your nails with yellow polish. Let dry. Use a fine paintbrush dipped in black polish to make two eyes and a mouth.

Lovely Ladybugs

Paint the bottom portion of each nail with red polish. Let dry. Paint the top of each nail with black polish. When dry, use a toothpick dipped in black to draw a line down the middle and to make black dots. Use another toothpick dipped in white to make eyes.

Perfect Pedicure

For feet's sake, give your tired toes, soles, and heels a beauty break.

1 Toe Prep

Remove any polish from your toenails.

2 Take the Plunge

Soak your feet in warm water for 5 minutes, then dry them with a towel.

3 Trim

Clip nails that are too long straight across with a pair of clippers. (Always clip toenails when they are wet. They are softer and easier to cut.)

4 Shape

Rub the emery board over the edges of the white parts of your toenails to shape them. (Don't round off the edges, or the nails could become ingrown.)

5 Brush Up

Rub the nailbrush behind the white parts of your toenails to remove any dirt or lint. Gently brush the tops of your nails to remove any dead skin from around the nails.

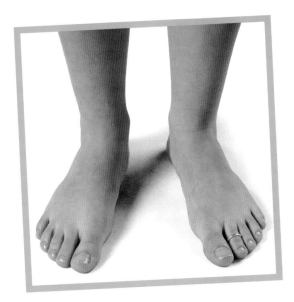

6 Moisten, Rub & Relax

Rub lotion onto your feet to ease dryness and to soften cuticles around your toenails. While applying lotion, take the tension right out of your toes and feet with a foot massage.

7 Buff or Polish

Use a toe separator, cotton balls, or crumpled-up tissues between your toes to keep them apart while you polish your toenails. Buff or paint each toenail, starting with the big toe and moving to the smallest.

Ingrown Nail

A nail can become ingrown when its corner grows into the skin alongside it. See a doctor if this happens to you. In the meantime, avoid wearing too-tight shoes, and ease the pain by soaking your foot in warm water. To prevent ingrown nails (and a doctor visit), trim and file your toenails straight across—not in a curved or oval shape.

Heel Healer

Is the skin on your heels dry and cracked? Rub on lots of lotion, then wear a pair of cotton socks for 30 minutes. Your feet will thank you!

Ooh-La-La Spa Party

Get the girls together for a day of facials, manicures, munchies, and giggles.

Dear Beth,
You have an appointment at Sabrina's Day Spa for an afternoon of facials, nail painting, and Fun!

Date: Oct. 11
Time: 2:00 pm
Bring your own bathrobe!

Beth Peters
148 Blossom Ln.
Haywood, CA

Spa Delights

Treat spa guests to healthy, yummy food. Blend yogurt and fresh or frozen fruit to make smoothies. Roll up sliced turkey and cheese in tortillas. Put out a tray of veggies and dip. Pour on the glitz with sparkling grape juice or make fruity spritzers by adding juice to sparkling water. Indulge with chocolate-covered strawberries for a sweet finale.

Get Crafty

Take a break from pampering yourselves and decorate hand-held mirrors with mini beads, sequins, or pom-poms. Or make rings for your fingers and toes by threading sparkly beads and buttons onto twist ties.

Spa Favors

Decorate small paper bags with ribbon handles and label them with your spa's name. Fill with nail decals, scented bath beads, cute hair thingies, and free perfume samples from the department store. Hand them out to guests as they leave—relaxed, refreshed, and happy.

Salon Scene

Make your party space perfect for pampering.

Manicure Bar

Set up a table and chairs and stock the table with manicure tools such as emery boards, soaking bowls, nail decals, and polish. Divide guests into pairs and have them take turns doing each other's nails.

Pedicure Corner

Set up a lounge chair for a do-it-yourself pedicure station. Place pedicure tools and a tub for foot soaks nearby. Tell each guest where to empty the water when she's done, so the next guest can start with clean water.

Facial Station

Take over the bathroom or set up a table just for freshening your faces. Set out handheld mirrors and soft towels. Mix up a batch of oatmeal smoothies (see page 20) for your guests' faces. And for that special spa touch, have a bowl of cucumber slices on hand to help soothe tired eyes.

Good Vibes

Tune the radio to soothing music, or play a relaxing CD.

Eye Candy

Have plenty of magazines, catalogues, and photo albums around for guests to page through while waiting for their nails to dry or their feet to soak.

Pillow Pad

Toss lots of pillows around the room and make the floor comfy and fun to lounge on.

Photo Ops

Get "before" and "after" shots of each guest. And be sure to get some in the middle, too—complete with cucumber slices and face masks on.

before

after!

Write to us!

How do you pamper yourself?
Do you have a special skin-care
routine? What's your favorite way
to paint your nails?
Send your secrets to:

Spa Editor
American Girl Library
Pleasant Company Publications
8400 Fairway Place
Middleton, WI 53562

Nail Decals

Decorating your nails is easy with stick-on decals.

To Apply:

1. Clean and dry nails thoroughly.

2. Polish or leave nails natural.

3. Choose a decal and peel it off the sheet.

4. Place decal on nail and press down gently.

5. Top with a coat of clear polish to seal and protect your decal.

To Remove:

Use nail polish remover.

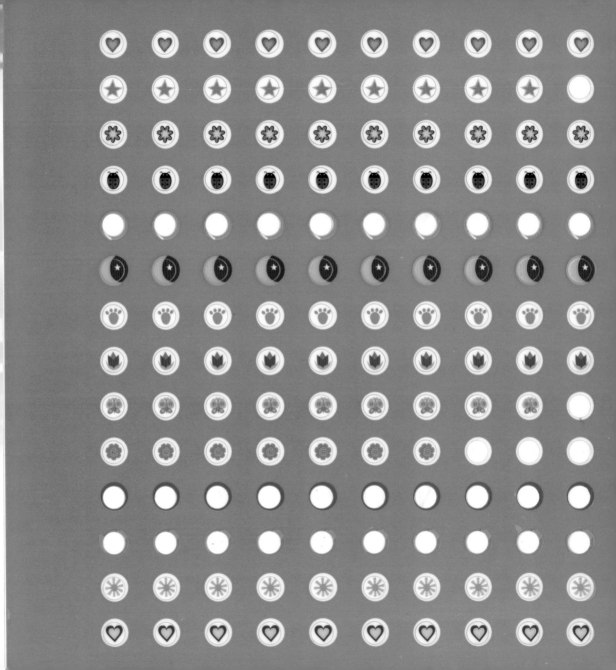